To Read a Poem

Meagan Jordan

Presentation by *BookLeaf Publishing*

Web: www.bookleafpub.com

E-mail: info@bookleafpub.com

ISBN: 9789395223751

First edition 2022

DEDICATION

To the people who love me.

ACKNOWLEDGEMENT

This adventure in writing has been an amazing experience, and I'm thankful to my family for being supportive. My oldest child Azriel for being a sounding board and keeping me company on the porch while I would write. Kyler and Tydus for being appreciative of my poems and letting me write instead of pestering me. And Tim for freeing up time for me to write by taking care of the kids and for loving me. Thank you Brandon for renewing my interest in writing and also for loving me. And to all of the above for being the inspiration for my poetic thoughts.

PREFACE

I chose to participate in a challenge to write at least one poem every day for 21 days. At first I wasn't sure what my poems would be about, but I ended up having to carry a notebook around with me or send texts to myself to keep track of all the things I thought were poetic. Included in this book are some of these writings, with themes ranging from emotions and relationships to daily life as a mom and cashier.
My list of what I want to write about just keeps growing, and I will definitely keep writing.

To Read a Poem

To see this tangible thing in your mind's eye
To feel what you'd feel if your eyes fell upon it
in truth
Words so vividly painted they're a work of art
But just to look upon the words is not enough
they must be brought to life by your own
imagination
To bring you, yourself
into the creation process and finish these
paintings with your mind
images that will never be the same for another
person
but always so beautiful
To read a poem is to join a poet in making
beauty

The Power of Words

Oh, the power that words do possess!
And remarkable what comes with their
comprehension.
Words are a cause to which there's an effect;
Speaking is done with specific intention.

A speaker wants others to listen,
But to hear them is never enough.
With those words always comes expectation;
Provoke thought, action, emotion, or even
rebuff.

A response given may be indirect.
Inadvertent consequences along with those
you'd expect.
Just the action of speaking itself,
The reaction of listening compels.

Those that listen have power as well,
To understand, learn, obey, or retell.
And words falling on ears that are deaf,
Withholds influence and makes for wasted
breath.

An Open Book

I open up my pages, let you in and let you read;
The story of the person I am laid out for you to
see.
If I choose to trust you with the secrets my pages
hold,
If I let the tale of who I truly am unfold;
How will you interpret what you see of who I
am?
Am I someone you could love? Will you truly
give a damn?
Or will you toss that book into a corner or the
trash?
How many chapters will you read before you
decide we clash?
Will you try to make me think you want to read
it all?
Is it really games you like? Do you want to see
me fall?
Or did you judge me by the cover and now you
are nonplussed?
Some genres aren't for everyone, find another
section if you must.

When An Artist Loves You

When an artist loves you
You inspire their everything
You unwittingly become a muse
And become part of songs they sing

In all things that move them they see your heart
It becomes apparent in their art
They cherish the images and feelings you bring
And long to transpose them into something
undying

No matter what form their works may take
Be it song, dance, drawing, poem, or paint
A part of you is in it too
Your love helped to make something new.

Melody and Harmony

Melody is a beautiful thing;
The part of a song most want to sing.
But some are drawn to the harmony;
The background voice that tends to bring
The best out of the song with sounds entwined,
Chords to emphasize
Resonance when notes combine,
To bring out more depth; a strain, divine!
And though to the background it sometimes
fades,
Not quite as noticed, it still pervades
And serves to complement the array,
Not needing the lime light, nor to just deviate.
Simply content with being the support,
With another earning the most report.
Though occasional acknowledgement is nice,
When one knows that some go unrecognized.
When someone comes along who sees
The accompaniment as an inspiring thing,
And knows what it takes to take the back seat
To play second chair
And be graciously aware
Of the importance of each little element;
And know that every part is relevant

In the making of the final masterpiece,
And sharing that essential emotional outlet it
brings.

A failed poem

I can't figure out what to write.
Is this what real poets feel like?
Does that line even actually rhyme?
How many syllables should it be this time?
I guess it doesn't hurt to try
But I'm not really a poet, I cannot lie.
Unless all it takes
Is to be someone that makes
A few lines that all rhyme and relate.

The Sky is Blue

What color is the sky you ask?
Why, blue of course!
A well-known fact.
But I suggest you look again,
It may be blue, it may be black.
Or perhaps it's white or gray;
The sky looks different every day.
Still, if questioned all will say
The sky is blue and this is true.

Please don't just let them tell you so,
Look for yourself so you will know.
It's red and pink, purple and yellow.
There's clouds, and snow,
even a rainbow.

And if you listen to the crowd
You might just miss it; look right now!
It's not enough to ask and listen,
See it and you'll be a witness.
And if asked then you can say
The sky can look any which way!

Sleeping Snail

Sleeping snail, please come out. All is well!
Surely outside conditions will satisfy.
"It's not safe out there, I'll sleep in my shell."

Tell me what I can do to compel.
It's lovely today, come look at the sky!
Sleeping snail, please come out. All is well!

The gardeners here no longer repel.
No reason to think you might die.
"It's not safe out there, I'll sleep in my shell."

Sleeping snail, please come out. All is well!
Rain has come, the ground isn't dry.
"It's not safe out there, I'll sleep in my shell."

You've slept so long, like you're under a spell!
Out here you'll find what you need if you try.
"It's not safe out there, I'll sleep in my shell."

Time slipped past and though nothing befell,
I plead again but heard the same reply;
Sleeping snail, please come out. All is well!
"It's not safe out there, I'll sleep in my shell."

Happiness?

Happiness in fleeting moments is easy to find;
A joke, a high, a special moment with someone
special;
The beautiful and the delicious- all give us a
quick taste
Of the delicacy that is happiness.

But how do we keep the taste on our tongues?
How do we make it our default mode; a state of
being?

Do we store up those satisfying moments to
bring joy when it's become scarce?
Or let ourselves endure a starvation of
contentment so the taste is that much sweeter
When finally achieved?

Does that equal out to more happiness, or does it
teach us to be attracted to the scarcity?
Must we learn to accept that this is all there is
for us?

Do you accept?

Empathy

What I feel when you're sad I wouldn't call
sadness.
It's a yearning to see you happy again; a hope
that I'm not the cause of your tears;
An understanding of what "sad" feels like and
how it affects every part of your day;
An indignation because you deserve so much
better.

What I feel when you're happy is more than just
happiness.
Pure joy to see a genuine smile on your face,
Pride and accomplishment if I help to put it
there, or camaraderie with whoever did;
Longing to make happiness a bigger part of your
life;
And even a slight fear in the knowledge that it
won't last.

When you're angry I feel many different
emotions;
Fear that I'll push you away if I caused it;
Displeasure towards the ones who wronged you;
An urge to change your mood however I can;
Anxiety that I may upset you more if not careful;

And pride in your sense of justice and ability to manage your emotions.

12

Shape of Emptiness

To miss someone is to feel an emptiness
A void in your being that's shaped exactly like them
Inability to be content with your current circumstance
Because of a strong need for their presence in it
That hole can never truly be filled
Though some things make it feel less empty
Only time can make the hole shrink
But it's still that shape no one else can fit in

Overwhelmed

I'm overwhelmed with a desperate need
Of which I don't even know the nature.
I feel helpless, hopeless, worthless
Burdensome, lonely, and useless.
Why go on? It feels like unnecessary suffering!
There are people who would hurt,
But would they actually be better off without
me?
In a never-ending cycle;
Pain is here and pain will come again.
I can only hold on until the pendulum swings the
other way.

Dawn Always Comes

It's my default setting, I always feel low.
Negative emotions constantly drag me down.
A rain cloud over my head endlessly pouring to
the ground.
Why is it so dark? I want to feel the sun's glow.

Unnecessary fear of allowing feelings to show,
So I wear a smile even when depression
abounds.
Poisonous Lily of the Valley forms a beautiful
flower crown.
My true thoughts and feelings they'll never
know.

No! You have people who care, so allow them to
show you.
If they only knew your burden they'd help make
it light.
No more holding it in, let your real feelings
come through.
With loving true friends there's no need for
fright.
The sun will shine and you can wear a smile
that's true.
Dawn always comes to put an end to the night.

Intricate

We've always fit together like the right puzzle
piece.
A smooth unbroken picture; can't even see a
crease.
Our puzzle shows a different picture now but
we're still a perfect fit.
No edges so we can keep growing, adding pieces
bit by bit.
Some people see the picture change and think
they no longer belong,
But we've got it figured out, for us at least,
that's wrong.

Though we change, we change together.
The way of things does ebb and flow,
But we know that we're forever,
Our love just continues to grow.

At times you go your own way, and I go mine
it's true
Our paths will always meet again no matter what
we do.
We walk life's path with each other, I know it's
meant to be.

Yet sometimes we go our separate ways to see
all there is to see.
But it never fails, we can't wait 'til we're
together again
To share the happiness we've found, a beautiful
compersion.

Though we change, we change together.
The way of things does ebb and flow,
But we know that we're forever,
Our love just continues to grow.

Our natural attraction is strong like gravity
It keeps our feet planted on the ground wherever
our hearts may be.
Around the world but back again, repelling
nothing, always open.
This pattern of our love goes on, a cycle never
broken.
Because we know love has no bounds, like the
universe it's infinite,
Our love, our life, our universe is incredibly
intricate.

Though we change, we change together.
The way of things does ebb and flow,
But we know that we're forever,
Our love just continues to grow.

Euphoria

On those euphoric occasions, stars align, we
make time
Our bodies entwine or simply your hand in mine
I know a blissful feeling of contentment
How deeply I'm loved in that moment
Nothing else matters for that short time
Until We have to go back to life, get on with the
grind
Until responsibilities cause us to part
And we spend time with others who also hold
our hearts
But still, always in the back of my mind
Are thoughts of you and those precious times
And I look forward to when we're together
again
Sharing drinks, making love, or conversation,
Music, food, games, or something new.
Whatever we do, I just want to be with you.

Compliments

Do you say it because it's true, or because you
love me and I'll be happy
If you do?
My love, I wish to make you happy because I
love you, and I love you
Because it's true.

A Weathered House

A weathered house, garden overgrown
Sits nestled in a field alone.
Though, in truth, alone it's not;
Smoke leaves the chimney, the fireplace is hot.

Warm inside those cracked-brick walls,
While ivy up the sides does crawl
A happy family lives their life,
Unbothered by insignificant strife.

That household learned a priceless lesson;
The important things in life. So listen
And I will share with you as well,
So you and yours can also dwell
Not in a house but in a home
And never feel that you're alone.

For even if your walls will rot,
And poverty becomes your lot
You'll know the secret and you'll be
Contended, though onlookers see
A house in shambles, broken down,
A kingdom that has lost its crown.

But I digress! I'll now return

To the secret that you wished to learn.
It's this; What truly makes us happy
Is love and family, whether that be
Family you're given, or family you choose
They are what you mustn't lose.

For having connections, and people you trust
Makes life worth living. Now you must
Take this knowledge and apply
The concept to your daily life.

Now look again at that house and find
Perhaps you've opened up your mind.
Can you see the hidden beauty?
The structure isn't important truly.
Any dwelling where love is shown
Is not just a house, it is a home.

Motherhood

They come to me for comfort in tough situations
And bombard me with requests and questions
that interrupt
But I love coming home to their happy faces
And compliments even when they're really
sucking up

I cherish the little differences in each personality
And the inherent love a child has for their
parents
I notice habits they certainly learned from me
And parts of their father I'd hoped they wouldn't
inherit

Half-squashed flowers picked for me just
because
Long-winded, detailed lectures about their
current interests
Drawings of the things they know I love
Hugs and kisses and bedtime wishes

It's not always easy to say the very least
But the little things make being a mom
worthwhile
Without them my life would never be complete

There is no love like that of a mother for her
child

Customer Service & Don't Be That Guy

Customer Service

Good morning, I'm fine. How are you?
Thanks for calling, anything I can do?
I appreciate your patience.
My apologies for the inconvenience.
Let me know if you need help.
Please come again soon!

Don't Be That Guy

The extra mile is what you expect,
Yet you're already rude as you walk in the door.
The pay's not enough, I don't owe you a speck.
Dude, get the fuck outta my store!

To My Younger Self

Young child, afraid to speak up
Walking on eggshells
Mustn't ever interrupt
Don't be a burden
They're going through enough

Do what's right
Do what you're told
Believe only this
You must fit the mold

Fail and lose your worth
You'll set them off
You'll make things worse
It's really your own fault
You're the one that is perverse

Wait…

Now that you've grown you're starting to open
up;
To speak your feelings and needs and voice how
you should be loved.
That part of you served a purpose, you don't
need to be ashamed.

That child did what they had to do to get through
and should be acclaimed!

But now you can recognize that it's ok to be
heard.
It's ok to have opinions, beliefs, and feelings
that don't defer!
It doesn't really mean that you're broken or
you've strayed
Just because you choose to live your life a
different way.

You can make you own choices and be who you
want to be;
Love who you want to love; Speak when you
want to speak.
They might not like it, but it's true that if they
love you for you
They'll accept who you've become and love you
still no matter what.

So keep learning how to be yourself. Live your
life and live it well!
And still remember your inner child, let them
out once in a while.
They deserve to see the you they helped to
make, they helped get through.
And to enjoy that newfound voice and that
beautiful freedom of choice.

A Haiku Page

Adorable snail
I want to follow your trail
But it twists and turns

Lovely gibbous moon
Hiding behind gnarled branches
A sight to behold

Such precious feelings
Of overwhelming passion
And intimacy

Do I look like that?
The angles of a photo
Different perspectives

A love of reading
Images fly from the page
Take me somewhere new

A higher purpose
Make life better for others
Starting with my kids

www.ingramcontent.com/pod-product-compliance
Lightning Source LLC
LaVergne TN
LVHW021335200726
843509LV00014B/2537